Little Things Shared

ALSO BY SUSAN NEWMAN

BOOKS

Little Things Mean a Lot:
Creating Happy Memories with Your Grandchildren

Little Things Long Remembered:
Making Your Children Feel Special Every Day

Parenting an Only Child:
The Joys and Challenges of Raising Your One and Only

Getting Your Child into College:
What Parents Must Know

Let's Always…
Promises to Make Love Last

Never Say Yes to a Stranger:
What Your Child Must Know to Stay Safe

You Can Say No to a Drink or a Drug:
What Every Kid Should Know

It Won't Happen to Me:
True Stories of Teen Alcohol and Drug Abuse

Don't Be S.A.D.:
A Teenage Guide to <u>S</u>tress, <u>A</u>nxiety & <u>D</u>epression

Memorable Birthdays:
Now a Guide…Later a Gift

VIDEOTAPES

Never Say Yes to a Stranger

You Can Say No to a Drink or a Drug

It Won't Happen to Me

Don't Be S.A.D.

Little Things Shared

Lasting Connections Between
Family and Friends

Susan Newman, Ph.D.
author of *Little Things Mean a Lot*

Illustrations by Cary McIver

Crown Publishers, Inc.
New York

Published by Crown Publishers, Inc.,
201 East 50th Street, New York, New York 10022.
Member of the Crown Publishing Group.

Random House, Inc. New York, Toronto, London, Sydney, Auckland
www.randomhouse.com

CROWN and colophon are trademarks of Crown Publishers, Inc.

Printed in the United States of America

Design by Laura Rose

Library of Congress Cataloging-in-Publication Data
Newman, Susan.
Little things shared : lasting connections between family and friends /
Susan Newman.—1st ed.
1. Family—United States.   2. Family reunions—United States.
3. Communication in the family—United States.   I. Title.
HQ536.N525   1998
306.85′0973—dc21   97-28721

ISBN 0-517-70821-3

10   9   8   7   6   5   4   3   2   1

First Edition

For my family and friends,
who taught me how to stay
closely connected

❧ Contents ❧

❧ Author's Note ❧

LITTLE THINGS SHARED evolved from a very personal concern. My immediate family is quite small, and "first-string" aunts, uncles, and cousins live in other parts of the country. As a result, I wonder and worry about my son's family connection. Who will be there for him as his parents age? Where will he gain a history of his family, a sense of who he is?

This book was designed, in part, to help my son find distant relatives who may be able to fill a historical gap, but also to give you and your children a better understanding of who you are. You'll recognize how exciting it is to be with or to find someone very much like yourself, someone with whom you have instant rapport because of familial ties, someone you want to be with because he or she has so much to share with you.

You'll be surprised how supportive extended family and close friends can be in ways you probably never considered. For those with children, you'll get many ideas on how to interest them in keeping family foremost and forever significant. For those without children, you'll learn how to keep your ties strong, and most important, you'll have the tools you need to be active within the family. You'll discover adventuresome and novel ways for connecting with both immediate and distant family members and close friends. All in all, you will learn how to be a better relative and friend.

❧ Connecting ❧

NOT TOO LONG AGO, connecting with relatives was unnecessary. Both your immediate and extended family lived in the same area, often in the same house. Family members watched over one another on a daily basis and helped with everything from raising the children to razing the barn or building your home.

In the past few generations, children have been raised to be independent, to go off on their own. Society has emphasized and valued separation from family, but there's a strong trend toward renewing the option to relate, to get close again.

Technology encourages close family connections. You can not only reach family members instantly, but you can also discover and locate relatives you may never knew you had—generally easily and quickly. Finding them opens new vistas of exploration and fascination. You may discover more people you feel comfortable with and can rely on. The fact remains that, more often than not, when things go wrong, family members are the people you count on. They are the ones you probably depend on, along with a few very close friends.

Many people have made adjustments when deciding who is family. Because of divorce, families are more complicated, broader in many respects. Some family trees have branches grafted in myriad directions, allowing more and more options for an extended family.

Those families that have escaped divorce and have followed the trend to have fewer children have extended their families in other ways. They seek out distant relatives and include them in their small circle; they substitute friends in key roles traditionally held by family. When you make family and your exceptional friends a priority, wondrous and exciting developments evolve.

There's a lot to learn about building bonds by following the advice and feelings others have about their families. You will find many, many ways to connect beyond the usual weddings, holidays, and funerals.

Ideally, this book will cause you to reflect on your role in the family, and, perhaps, alter or expand it. Above all else, family is heartening, comforting, and surprising, and before you have read very far, you will begin to understand the importance of putting family first.

Little Things Shared

FAMILY FINDS

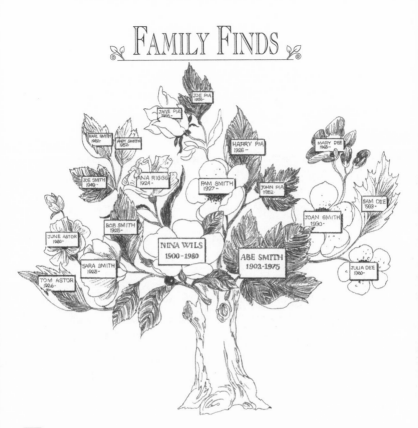

Family is about ties and knowing your roots. People are curious in different ways and have very individual reasons for exploring their lineage. For some, there are holes in the past, perhaps painful ones, that they would like to fill. For others, a face-to-face bridges gaps, closes a chapter in their lives, strengthens fragile bonds, or is the wonderful beginning of relationships they've missed.

WHY SEARCH?

Someone Like Me

"I adored my grandmother more than any other person in our family. I've been thinking about visiting Budapest because she was from that area. I wonder if any of my grandmother's descendants still live there. I'd like to find someone else in the family besides myself who has her zest for living and zany nature," explains Anita.

Medical Alert

Meredith, on the other hand, wants to know her medical history. "There's a lot of cancer in my family, but I don't know how widespread and what kinds."

According to a leading research physician, "If you are aware of your family's health history you may be able to attend to prevention and/or early detection for yourself or your children. But," he warns, "a cluster of a disease in one family does not necessarily mean that illness is genetic. Such clusters can happen by pure chance."

Lone Relative

Gretchen searches because her parents are dead. "I have only one aunt alive and she's in her late seventies. I must have more relatives somewhere; I don't want to be alone," she admits.

The Other Side

William knew his family roots dated back more than two hundred years in this country, but, as he says, "I felt my son should know his Jewish side, that's my wife's side of the family—where they came from, what their lives had been like, and who they were."

Discoveries

"As a first-generation American, most of my family history starts abruptly in the 1930s. Before that, there is nothing written or documented. Like many others in the same position, I am curious about my past," states Richard.

Where Did My Nose Come From?

The first thing people look for in relatives is physical similarities. Many people, not seeing the origin in their immediate family, want to know where their chins come from or the source of their height.

"I was adopted at birth," says Jonathan, age twenty-five. "I located then arranged to see my birth mother. She gathered the children she had later in life and her father for the occasion. Everyone was short. The males were under five-seven and the females were really small—five-three and under. I looked around the room and knew I had inherited the short gene from my grandfather. Everyone in my adopted family is big. For once, I, at five-eight, was a giant," jokes Jonathan.

Surprising Similarities

Beyond the physical, Talia sought out her grandfather because, in her words, "I knew he was a rotten person. After all, he left my grandmother with two small children and no money to raise them. But I still wanted to know who he was. I believe strongly in nature over nurture. Meeting my grandfather for the first time at age thirty explained some things about myself that didn't come from the rest of my family.

"I inherited my 'artistic eye' and compulsive neatness from him. His paintings were quite good, but what shocked me was that he keeps his cookbooks and videos in alphabetical order. I do that with my books, too," confesses Talia.

He's My Brother

Not every discovery must be positive and pleasurable, as Fredda learned. "We remet after twenty-seven years of not seeing each other. I'm glad I went to the trouble to find my brother because it reinforced the fact that you don't have to like all of your relatives."

Curiosity Satisfied

"Once I found my estranged uncle," Frederick says, "I kept up with him and his family for several years. It was important for me to know him even if it didn't become a close bond. I learned about other members of my family."

Reassurance

"One of the jokes in my family is that we all like to talk too much," rambles Claire, who recently visited a group of West Coast relatives she hadn't seen since childhood. "Suddenly, talking too much no longer seemed like some sort of personality defect to me, but rather a humorous family trait. I didn't feel so peculiar anymore."

Expanding Roots

You may just be inquisitive, wanting only to know who your relatives are and how they are connected, or it may be something more—as it was in Glenda's case. "I was an illegitimate child, adopted at birth. Once I found my natural mother, I learned that I had a huge family. I wanted to be acquainted with each person in it. I want to be part of that family as well as my adopted family."

Not So Small

"When the subject came up, I had always said, 'I have a very small family.' Once I began looking for relatives, I learned that we are quite a sizable group. That was not only a revelation but also very consoling as I got older. I've been in touch with many of them and we plan to meet when I go west on vacation.

"I feel safer, protected," admits Otto, who is approaching his fiftieth birthday. "So much for my 'poor me' small family speech."

Puzzle Parts

Meeting family gives you the inside track on things you may have wondered about while growing up. Wendy recalls visits from one of her mother's cousins.

"We were all astonished by this woman, Cousin Annie, who visited and wore a very tight pink suit. As little girls, my sisters and I

were so struck with how pretty she was; we wanted her to come and spend the night at our house, but she never did. Twenty years later I still remember that pink suit and her long legs with her feet perched in very high, skinny heels. Cousin Annie was a 'professional,' as our mother used to say. We finally know *what* profession!"

Very Interesting

If you are out of touch with family, you can't know who in your family is doing something that is interesting. "I had avoided family reunions until last year. I discovered that most of my cousins, especially the ones I hadn't met, are doing quite remarkable things," reveals Ben. "One's a helicopter traffic reporter for a television news program; another is working on cancer research; and one just became an FBI agent. What they had to say was fascinating."

Support in Low Moments

"My family is engaging," says Jane, "because the women are so strong; they were pushing the frontiers quite literally.

"One of my great-great-grandmothers was convicted of being a witch in the Salem witch trials. She escaped from prison at the age of seventy-eight. I see the strength of these women. You would not think that knowledge would be useful in present reality, but in my low moments, I think of my great-great-grandmother and say to myself 'I can do that,' whatever *that* is at the time. I'm not from a bunch of wusses, and that's nice to know."

Missed Opportunity

"My family connections are filled with regrets. I don't know how we managed to isolate ourselves so much, but we did. I was chatting about my aunt Ida, and my son, who is twenty-three years old, looked at me in all seriousness and said, 'Who is Aunt Ida?'

"Aunt Ida is my mother's younger and only sister, my child's only great-aunt. I was horrified. I knew I had to reestablish relationships," laments Faith.

Lighting a Fire

"A man called me out of the blue and announced he thought he was a relative of mine—a second cousin. He kindled something in me and I started making phone calls based on the names he gave me and names I remembered. Other cousins gave me names I had forgotten.

"The best way I can sum it up is that the whole process snowballed," comments Joe, who began a family search that continued for five years. "Now I know where I came from, and that's very meaningful and reassuring."

A Game of Sorts

"I began searching just for fun," reports Laura. "I wasn't looking for anyone in particular—I just thought it would be interesting; the excitement of the hunt. Finding relatives is an intellectual exercise for me and tremendously rewarding. I feel triumphant once I've made a connection."

Proud to Be Me

Meeting family for the first time or after years of "separation" offers a lot of affirmation of who you are by seeing where you came from. As Gunther proclaims, "It makes me proud."

The Future

Life changes. Fun-filled days and tight bonds with relatives you may not have known existed are always very real possibilities.

Searching Facts

It's NEVER TOO LATE to start pulling family together. If the generations that preceded you are or were passive about the family, take over.

These days it isn't too difficult to find a relative or your roots. It takes time and persistence to reconstruct history, yes, but most search elements are accessible in one form or another: from photographs of the ships relatives arrived on when coming to this country to marriage licenses and old people still living in your family's village of origin.

Working Backward

The rule of thumb is to start with what you know, then speak with relatives, the eldest first. Don't assume you know everything.

Have them tell you about every single relative they can remember. Ask lots of questions about places, connections, memories—and get it all down on paper.

For Posterity

Take notes or record conversations. Request telephone numbers or addresses your relatives may have so that you or someone else in your family can contact your "family finds." You need the person's full name and the last place anyone knew he or she lived. Where they were born and date of birth could also be a crucial piece in your search.

Idle Conversation

"Years ago when I lived in Holland, I mentioned to my cousin Stella that I was going to Paris on business. She said, 'You're going to see Cousin Fran, aren't you?' I said, 'I don't have a Cousin Fran.' 'Sure you do,' she insisted, and proceeded to tell me how I was related to Fran, who turned out to be a first cousin by marriage. I've seen Fran for twenty years now and we're very fond of each other. If I hadn't mentioned that business trip I never would have known I had a cousin in Paris." Fran shrugs at the tenuous nature of happenstance.

Records

Marriage licenses and divorce records are full of good search information and, depending on the state in which the divorce was granted, the records will show an employer, property owned, and Social Security numbers.

Minor and Major Alterations

Over the decades, the spelling of names often changes, and many names were completely changed when people arrived in America—two factors that might complicate your search. Some changes are minor, such as Mabry to Mayberry or Maybrey; others more dramatic, and hence more difficult to trace. Levinsohn, in one family, was changed to Martin. Ideally, someone in the family will remember a change took place and will know the original family name.

Clues Everywhere

Most states have entered all births and marriages of the past fifty years in databases so that they are available for searches with your computer. There are military as well as draft records that have a lot of personal information, even if the person did not serve. The New York Public Library has a wealth of information, as do the National Archives in Washington and its thirteen regional offices.

Help for Hire

There are individuals and organizations that specialize in genealogical searches. Once hired, they can piece together your family history.

Searching Tools

DESPITE THE FACT that families are smaller now than in previous generations, your ancestors probably had large families, leaving you much to discover. Whether you are looking to expand your family with living relatives, attempting to trace your heritage, or creating a social history for your family, multiple sources are available.

Where to Begin?

If you think your family arrived originally in New England, the 1790 census is the place to start. Early census taking, however, only included the name of the male head of the household.

Records Hold History

The Church of Latter-Day Saints, also referred to as the Mormon Church, has microfilmed original documents of genealogical importance—birth, death, and marriage records, as well as naturalization and military records—for every country they have been allowed to enter (most recently Russia and Belarus). Every twenty years they also put tax and census records on microfilm. These records of almost everyone who has ever lived, collected by the Mormons from all over the world, offer a pretty complete history of a family.

Passenger Cards

The National Archives has on microfilm the passenger cards for everyone who emigrated to this country between 1904 and 1940. Some passenger cards will tell you the town and/or country your relative arrived from. The cards were mircofilmed during the Depression, when many Americans were out of work and needed a job. Passenger cards have not been indexed prior to 1904.

Let Your Fingers Do the Walking

The most logical springboard for a search is the telephone book. Check it for relatives when you are out of town. Someone you reach may know the person you are looking for.

Volunteer Assistance

Volunteer organizations such as the American Red Cross and the Jewish Board of Family and Children Services will check phone books, military records, and Social Security offices for you at no charge. You don't have to be Jewish to ask for help from Family and Children Services.

Note: Social Security records for the United States, including applications, are available beginning in 1937.

Alumni Sources

If you know the high school, college, or university a relative attended, check with its alumni office. Many schools have alumni information on the Internet. Ask a classmate or classmate's parents. Often one tip leads to another, whether you are looking for a relative or a friend.

Graveyard Pointers

Cemetery records provide ages and birth dates you may be missing. Find out who in your family pays the grave maintenance fees. Through the bill, you can go to the correct records immediately.

The Advertisement

Advertise in a genealogical magazine for information about the village your grandparents came from as well as for information about specific people. Ads can also be placed on genealogical search sites on the Internet.

World Wide Web Searches and Sources

The best place to begin is with one of the many on-line guides, such as *George Archer's Genealogist's Guide to the Internet* or *The National Genealogical Society's Web Page*.

On-line guides direct you to genealogical libraries and information ranging from French, Italian, Dutch, Hungarian, and German genealogy to Internet newsgroups pertaining to African-American, Hispanic, Nordic, and Australian ancestry—virtually any ethnic group or country. You can go on-line to look for particular surnames, adoption data, ancestral locations. There are specific search sites pertaining to the Holocaust.

On-line you'll also find lists of magazines, libraries, and bookstores devoted to the subject, individual family home pages, and instructions on how to create a genealogical home page for your own family.

New Databases

Genealogy on the Internet is exploding. "It seems as if there's a new database every few days," remarks Nelson, who is in the middle of researching his heritage. "The newest allows you to enter the town you are looking for and it tells you exactly where the records are kept for that town. This saves years of looking!

"And," he adds, "it allows people who can't afford it or are too old to travel out of the country to discover family links."

Listings.com

Internet sites display free bulletin boards, many geared to specific nationalities, for posting what you know about a family member you wish to find or for requesting genealogical information:

THE MISSING LINK

Looking for information on Taylor family. Grandfather, Tyler, born 1895, in MA, married to Edith Winsor, 1924. Tyler and Edith had four children, all born in MA: Paul, Delilah, Clark, Jean.

Delilah, my mother, and Jean, my aunt, believe Paul and Clark have Winsor family history information. Any word on Paul or Clark Taylor would be greatly appreciated. Sisters lost touch after family misunderstanding.

Free Addresses

You can also access mailing lists: listings for government agencies and associations (pharmacists, obstetricians, accountants, lawyers, etc.); law and information exchange sites for adoptees; and places to look for missing persons. Unlike telephone company information, these lists give telephone numbers *plus addresses* at no charge. Some sites claim to search and respond via e-mail within forty-eight hours.

A Head Start

"My aunt had made a genealogy for one side of our family that dated back to 1799," explains Ted. "When she gave it to me, I felt as if she had given me a very important gift. It became my most valuable tool when I decided to search my ancestry back one generation further."

Preserving Family

Family is forever in flux. Members are discovered; members die; members are born. As a result, family history is always a work in progress—one that needs to be preserved.

In all likelihood you are not as fortunate as Sam, who has a thousand-page book, handwritten by his grandfather, which he has had translated. It tells the family history in Russia from 1885 to 1965. Sam feels that "by writing about himself and his family, my grandfather lives on."

Family ties and family history have been maintained in many forms: pictures stored in shoe boxes or handsomely labeled albums, books organized by computer publishing programs or typeset and printed by professional printers, handwritten and oral stories passed from generation to generation. In any form, preservation is a celebration of ancestry—a connection between the past and the present.

Continuity Sought

"After being confronted with a life-threatening illness, I realized that my life no longer stretched aimlessly in front of me," discloses Polly, who is in her fifties. "The illness made me think about my family and what I wanted to let my children know about me, about my relatives, and about our history together."

Details, Details

Your family record—be it a self-published book or stapled sheets of paper—may include everything from how holidays were celebrated in your family's country of origin, diet, the professions of family members, laws, and descriptions of their hometown to dilemmas in leaving their country, escape techniques, and paths to arrival in the New World. Digging is required to find the particulars. You may want to prepare a list of questions before you speak with relatives.

Past Explains Present

Was there a classical pianist in the family? A saxophone player? An artist? A tailor? Successful businessperson?

Who had what blood type? Who died of what and at what ages? How tall was great-grandfather? How many siblings did grandmother have?

Family history is multifaceted and often explains the next generation's preferences and inclinations. It may be helpful in understanding mental or health problems.

Making the Rounds

Send a blank book from family member to family member requesting that they record any bit of family history they would like. Give them a few examples to get them started, such as those below. The first is from the Levys' bound text; the second, from notes attached to the Peals' family tree:

My father was one of 6 children. Only he and my uncle Carl were born in the United States. The others were born in Vilna, Russia (Lithuania). Three children died before my grandparents came to America. The ones who survived and lived here are Uncle Carl, Aunt Sadie, and my father, Jack.

Uncle Billy suffered from what, at the time, was called dementia praecox or schizophrenia. It is said that he heard voices. Uncle Billy committed suicide at age 26. He was found in a hotel room with the gas jets on.

Meeting Opposition

You may encounter resistance. While some older relatives will talk incessantly about the past; others are reluctant to open up about family matters. For those who are closed off, ask directed questions to warm them up: What did you do for fun when you were a child? Where did you live when you were a child? What was your favorite meal? Tell me about the first car you drove. And so on. You are asking for stories rather than specifics. As your relative begins to reminisce, family names and facts will work their way into the conversation.

Journal Entries

Keep a journal or notebook. At every opportunity add facts as you receive or remember them. Eventually it will become a valuable series of recollections to leave as a legacy to the family that will follow you. Give as much detail of your family's roots and lives as you know. A grandchild will delight in knowing that his great-grandfather spoke several languages, thus explaining, in part, his own interest in languages.

This journal entry, taken from one woman's diary, makes it clear why the writer's mother's home was antiseptically clean:

Your great-grandmother was not a good housekeeper. Her beds had bedbugs and lice; there were cockroaches behind the wallpaper. It's no surprise that your grandmother is very fearful of bugs. She kept our house spotless. She spent most of her time cleaning.

Personal Nuggets

Bits of your life will engage your children. You can sprinkle them with humor, as Lois did in notes to her children:

I got my driver's license when I turned sixteen. It gave me great freedom. I drove around with my friends at night to "spy" on the houses of boys we had crushes on. Sometimes we would wear Mickey Mouse and Donald Duck or Peter Rabbit masks. It's a wonder the police never stopped us.

Hampton chose to record what he called his father's unending "songs":

Close the door. Talk is cheap. Clean up your room. You can marry rich as easily as poor. I'm not caring for any grandchildren—I've already done my time.

The Committed Historian

Save letters from family members that discuss what different people in a nuclear family are doing. Over the years you will have created a sense of family history. Ask members of your family to forward family letters to you for storage.

History in Photographs

Keep old photographs safe in protective plastic sheets or albums. New family photos should be stored just as carefully because they, too, will have historic value before you know it. Date your photographs if they do not come from the photo processor with dates on them.

Searching for Ancestors

Send a letter out to all members of the family asking for old photographs of relatives they may have stored in basements and attics.

Place in Time

Ask older members of the family to identify and date, if possible, your vintage family photos. As time passes, fewer and fewer people will be able to recognize those from previous generations.

Unidentified

Whenever the family is together display pictures of great-grandparents and great-aunts and -uncles to see if anyone can add a name or pinpoint where a relative came from.

For the Curious

Take tidbits of information and an assortment of ancestral family photos and write a book about your family's heritage.

Photo Log

"I hit a gold mine in my grandmother's attic—decades of photos stored in shoe boxes. I took them all and had them scanned onto videotape. For Christmas one year I gave each family member a copy of the tape. It was the best gift they got," boasts Gordon immodestly.

Colorized

"I gathered photos of my aunts and uncles when they were children. There was only black and white then. I colored in a tie, a dress sash, a bonnet, something on each picture, and then added humorous captions. There were about thirty photos, which I copied and bound for each of my aunts and uncles," says Bradley, a dentist whose hobby is painting.

Video Log

"My niece recorded our family history as a food fete. She took hours and hours of footage, taped over many years, but used only the sections in which we were cooking, eating, or clearing up after a meal. All the scenes revolve around food. It's quite amusing and clever," says Lillian with admiration in her voice for her niece's ingenuity.

Family Fare

Most families have a food history, stories about meals or "standout" dishes that have been handed down for generations. Keep food history alive in your family by repeating stories like these at family gatherings:

- "My grandmother used to make rice wine," says Elyse. "She fermented it in the cellar. It tasted so nasty. I think I had one sip in my whole life, but it's part of who my grandmother was and how I remember her."

- "In my family, a holiday dinner must end with my great-grandmother's apple pie. The discussion is always around who re-creates it best—my mother or my grandmother," chuckles Raymond. "Since my grandmother is dead, you know what I say."

Susan's Recipe Box

"My boys are grown and live alone. I put recipes that are part of their heritage in an accordion folder with labeled sections for appetizers, desserts, and so forth. It's a family history, because I not only included recipes they loved while growing up but also recipes that belonged to my mother, grandmothers, aunts, and good friends.

"Each recipe was credited to its source and I added comments, such as, 'Eat this on New Year's Eve and you will have good luck the rest of the year'; 'We ate this in Italy when you boys were young'; and 'My mother fixed salmon croquettes on Thursday nights and served them with macaroni and cheese.'

"Now they can reminisce, have a cocktail party, fix Thanksgiving dinner, or just pig out," concludes Susan.

Just Desserts

Circulate forms requesting recipes, who in the family served them, and some reminiscences about the originators of the recipes. Then turn the collection, including personal comments, into a family cookbook.

You can ask for dessert recipes only and title the cookbook *Just Desserts from the [Name] Family* or leave the recipe choice open to anything from appetizers to desserts. In that case call your collection *The [Name] Family Fare* or *Three Generations of [Family Name] Recipes*.

Use a photograph from a family picnic, reunion, or celebration for the cover. Be sure to include a photo key of who's who.

Quilting Bee

Preserve family in a quilt. Squares might represent the birth of each child, the place you hold your reunion, and/or other significant family events and milestones. The quilting can be done during the year and the squares brought to a wedding, birthday celebration, holiday gathering, or family reunion.

The squares, once there are enough to be a quilt, can reside with the oldest family member or the person who has offered to sew them together.

Stir Fry

Pass along single recipe discoveries to the other cooks in your family and to your friends. By including your name on the recipe you are adding to or beginning your family's culinary history.

The Family Tree

WHETHER YOU BEGIN a few generations back or in the 1600s, family histories give a sense of the past, and in doing so provide important links to the present. Time passes quickly and family roots can easily be lost if not recorded in some way. Preparing a family tree is exciting, interesting, and can involve all family members who supply a name, a town, or other nugget of family lore that makes the tree a perfect replica of your family's connections.

A Variety

✿ "I have a family tree that includes two hundred twenty names all of whom originated from one great-grandfather who had six children," brags William.

✿ "My mother and I began tracing the family in the 1940s. We have a family tree for each side going back to 1632 with long descriptions," says Alice, who is in her seventies. "We have pages and pages that we keep in binders."

✿ Nancy is in awe of her cousin's work: "My cousin made a family tree, dug up pictures and photographs and put together an amazing album. I love looking at it."

Growing a Family Tree

Once you have a few names and addresses, send letters informing relatives of your project. A few people will get really excited and immediately call you. Sending letters gets people thinking, but "calling is better," says Peter. "It forces them to talk to you. In my experience, most of the letters are ignored, but people were very receptive to my calls."

Branch by Branch

When gathering information for a family tree, limit yourself to one section of the family at a time. Rodney provides a valuable lesson: "I was doing all four sides of my wife's and my family's at the same time. The project became totally unwieldy. I stopped for a few years before beginning again with just my paternal grandfather's offspring. This much I can handle," he says and laughs.

Roadblocks

Some things in a family's history will always remain a mystery. If you get discouraged, stop searching for a period of time, then begin again when the mood strikes you, be that a few weeks, months, or years later. But don't give up because some elements cannot be tracked.

The Prize

For those researching a pilgrim family or an immigrant family of the late nineteenth or twentieth century there's even a family history writing contest held annually. The winner gets an expense-paid trip to the National Genealogical Society's yearly meeting, and the histories that demonstrate superior research skills, original documentation, and unusual format are submitted to a genealogical magazine for publication. Check the National Genealogical Society website for complete contest details.

Showing Off

Register your family tree on a family page website. You may discover other family pages with the same last name. Check them to see if there are relative overlaps.

From Simple to Elaborate

The family tree can be a list of names on a page or two or a simple set of connected lines and boxes with names and a few dates. The basic tree becomes information-packed by adding addresses, birth and death dates, and stories. It can become so involved and retroactive that it fills volumes.

Kinship Report

Once family data are entered into a computer with a genealogy software program, it can spit out all arrangements of kin. Click the mouse to discover how you're related to someone—third cousin three times removed, for instance.

While in progress or when completed, the family tree can be circulated on the Internet or by mail.

Trees with Artwork and Audio

Computer software programs also open creative options from scanning in photographs and artwork to adding video and sound.

A Tree Provides Leads

"I knew his name from our family tree. When I saw his name again listed as a guest at a convention I was attending I called his room and said, "Hi, Paul, I think you're my cousin."

A detailed family tree supplies names of many relatives you may not know. From it, you can build wonderful new relationships. Paul and his cousin have taken many trips together since they found each other, and their wives and children have become quite close.

TOUCHING BASE

Anyone, of any age, can take the initiative for keeping family close, but keeping up is hard to do. Amid the demands of daily life and the natural course of events you can easily lose track of family not involved in your day-to-day life. On top of normal pressures, staying in touch can simply be inconvenient. Yet, with Internet e-mail and the telephone, touching base is easier and more fun than ever.

As you will see, the energy expended to connect or be with family is worth the good feelings, satisfaction, and interesting, sometimes startling, facts gleaned from family and family gatherings. It's your job to let others know you care, that you are a part of them and they, in turn, are a part of you.

Out of Sight, Not Out of Mind

Don't be put off because you live far from a sibling or other relative who is important to you. Distance can enhance relationships with relatives. "When my brother moved to the other side of the country, we stopped taking each other for granted. When he was a few miles away, I didn't see him that often. Out of range, we both make an effort, and as a result, we are very close," declares Carl.

Personal Mission

Make it your mission to keep the family together, especially if you live away from your extended family. Call regularly; send younger family members birthday packages and holiday surprises.

Feeling as Motivation

Because of his strong memories, it's vital to John to maintain his connections to family: "I have a young child and I very much want her to be part of the families that were an integral part of my childhood. I like these people. I care about them. I like to spend time with them. I don't want my ties to the family to evaporate into nothing. My daughter is an only child and she'd be isolated, in a family sense, without these relationships."

Extra! Extra!

News is news no matter how it's presented. Read all about family matters in a newsletter. A letter about your nuclear family, typically sent around the holidays, can go out any "off" time of year. Rather than getting lost in the holiday bustle, it is more likely to be read and absorbed in March or May.

Newsletter tips: Don't fall into the trap of thinking that no one cares. People want to know what you and your family are doing. Your letter doesn't have to be clever or cute. It can be all text or spotted with photographs and art.

Young children can draw the pictures; adults supply the text. Your teenager can put it together with each family member adding a personal paragraph.

News for the Ages

Save newsletters in a file or on disk for review years—maybe decades—from now.

Hello, Hello

Arrange a monthly family conference call, a quarterly call, or one a year—perhaps timed for an anniversary or someone's birthday.

New Ties

If you discover relatives via the Internet, make plans to meet them if you are visiting or in their area on business. Bring along pictures and papers that may be of interest. In the final analysis, even if you end up only trading e-mail occasionally, it's a family connection you didn't have before.

Kindred Spirits

Set time aside for a relative with whom you have a strong bond or parallel interests. When family is together, make a point to see that person alone for breakfast or lunch—away from the others. Take a long walk or meet before everyone gathers—just the two of you.

Family Day

We celebrate Mother's Day, Father's Day, and, increasingly, Grandparents' Day. Choose a day—or more—and designate it Family Day. It's a day to contact relatives you haven't seen or spoken with in a long time.

For a Change

Have one of your children make the call or write a note to relatives or old friends.

LITTLE THINGS

Small Reminders

When you can't get together because of the miles that separate you, keep childhood memories alive. "My daughter's favorite cookies were, and still are, Oreos. One time I sent her an Oreo cookie tin; another time mugs with the Oreo logo for her, her husband, and her children," reports Eden.

Get Well

Send notes or call a relative who is ill or in the hospital as Warren did. "I did this for a cousin I didn't know that well—I only saw Frankie at reunions when we were kids—but I heard he was very ill and began corresponding with him.

"Years later when my dad got sick, Frankie went out of his way to come and visit with him. We developed a much closer relationship and appreciate each other, even though we are very different. His support is comforting."

Keep Calling

After the funeral, call periodically over an extended period of time to check on the mourner(s). They will be pleased that you have remained interested and concerned, especially if you "reside" on an offshoot branch of the family tree.

Batter Up

Be an avid sports fan for nieces, nephews, grandchildren, and children of good friends. Attend games and meets if you can, or call to wish them luck.

Precious Lamb

What began simply as an aunt giving her newborn nephew the affectionate nickname "Precious Lamb" has mushroomed into five decades of giving and receiving lamb-related items: lamb-shaped place mats, lamb salt and pepper shakers, lamb-theme artwork and dishes, etc. Recently, Precious Lamb sent his aunt a small stuffed toy lamb to keep her company when she woke up from surgery.

Close Confidant

If parent-child relationships are strained, make it possible for children to form alliances with another relative, someone they can talk to in place of a parent. Adolescents particularly will benefit from a sounding board in the form of a relative or friend who can listen to their problems and perhaps advise them in ways a parent can't.

Trickle-Down Effect

Plan trips together with a sibling's family and your spouse and children. By doing so you retain close, caring bonds over many decades. Adult feelings for each other will trickle down to the children. In the long run the cousins will respect one another and be concerned about one another's well-being.

Back and Forth

To make it more feasible for the family to be together and share time in relaxed circumstances, rotate holidays between parents' and siblings' homes. If you can, extend stays to make the time more meaningful.

Cementing Relationships

Use the children to repair unsatisfactory relationships you may have with a sibling. If you want cousins to be friends, get together for the sake of the children. You may discover that as adults you have a lot in common and the feelings you had as children are no longer so important.

Frequent Flyer

Use those extra mileage program coupons for a ticket to see someone you love or send the ticket so that a favorite relative or friend can spend time with you or with your children.

"What could be better," recalls Ariel, "than my cousins visiting Cleveland from South America and snow falling for two days in a row? Nothing," she answers her own question. "My mother dressed us warmly and we played outside for hours on end."

Head for the Hills

Take a sibling, niece or nephew, a parent, an aunt or uncle, or distant cousin you adore away for his or her birthday. You can go someplace close or someplace far away and exotic. Being together is the point, whether you're hiking the local terrain, sleeping at a campsite, or beaching it on a tropical island.

Rotation

"Every summer I have a niece or nephew visit us for a week. It allows me to get to know them better and builds a strong bond for my children with their cousins. Having one at a time gives us a chance to know them and them to know us," offers Heather.

Memory Enhancement

Create a story in poem form, date and identify, or caption each photo to record a relative's visit or an adventure you took together. Then send it on to him or her.

Local Produce

Is your region known for its great corn? Maple syrup? Delicious candy? Special cheese? Express mail a food, product, or trinket to friends and relatives that they can't get where they live.

College Shopping

When traveling with a college-bound child to look at schools to which she might apply, take time out to lunch or overnight with a relative you don't see often who lives en route or in the college's area.

Sharing Quarters

Share a vacation place with relatives and their offspring. Going away together solidifies family and forms close bonds.

Breaking the Barrier

Perhaps there's been a family feud that has nothing to do with you. It may have happened twenty years ago and almost everyone involved remembers nothing about it or is dead. Be the one to reconnect with those relatives you haven't known.

Home for the Holidays

Since immediate families are together for holidays such as Thanksgiving, Hanukkah, and Christmas, use the day before or the day after to merge family groups. On Friday or Saturday after Thanksgiving have a potluck supper with leftovers or Sunday brunch for the cousins and their children. It's your best shot to see *all* out-of-town relatives.

Snail Mail

The U.S. Post Office offers, as it always has, a perfect way—"snail mail" as computer aficionados call it—to keep family and friends informed and let them know you are thinking about them.

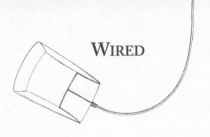

WIRED

Operating Instructions

"The four of us have stayed close by banding together from the time we were little girls," says Hillary, thirty-four, the oldest of four sisters. "Our mode of operation was always 'don't tell Mom and Dad anything that's troublesome.' Instead, we have a telephone hot line among ourselves and operate as each other's stabilizer. This was our principle in high school, but it really went into force when we started going to college and living apart. It's that way now that three of us are married and have new sets of problems. The kinds of things we talk about are better done interactively than by computer."

E-mail Strengthens Bonds

For those more electronically oriented, write a short paragraph in e-mail once or twice a week to keep your contacts strong.

E-mail: Another Perspective

If the relative you love doesn't let you off the telephone, if she's the type who must provide every detail of a story to the point that you can't stand to listen, e-mail's the answer. E-mail lets you remain in touch and not feel guilty, because you will no longer need to avoid the tedious phone calls.

Stranger No More

E-mailing is a great boon to relationships with nephews and nieces and others you might not normally stay in touch with. Send off an e-mail every few weeks and you'll be able to stay up to date on a nephew's school activities or his new job, his dating life, his interests. You can even ask him to deliver messages to other members of his family.

Finding Time

When you're responding to e-mail at home or at the office, drop a few lines to a relative in Bangkok, Scotland, Bethesda, Charleston, India, or Japan. You only pay your regular, usually monthly, Internet access charge; e-mail is free no matter where you send it.

Hello, Grandmother

The Bushes take advantage of worldwide technology. "My mother, who lives in Ireland," says Beatrice, "did not see her grown grandsons very often. So the boys and I decided to hook her up to the Internet. We bought her the necessary equipment for her eightieth birthday, then Bob, my older son, taught her how to e-mail. I send her an e-mail daily and she and the boys correspond about once a week. It just proves you're never too old." Or too far away.

Not Lost

E-mail allows you to keep in close contact with relatives you "discover" at reunions or when searching names for your family tree. "Now and then I e-mail relatives I found on the Internet—a cousin in Australia, a great-uncle in Phoenix—so we don't lose each other," comments Jay.

Informing Everyone

Once you make an e-mail address list in your Internet mailer, you can send the same message to everyone in your family with one click on the list. Inform them if you've discovered a member of the family or if you're planning a family party.

Up to Date

An e-mail once a month keeps family apprised of your activities and feeling attached. You can include pictures, movies, sounds, and links to other sites right in your e-mail. The receiver will see the images and hear the sound (which plays or automatically appears as an icon to click on) while scrolling your message.

Budding Artist

If you have a scanner, the equipment you need to copy pictures and artwork into your computer, then send one of your child's drawings via e-mail. Aunts, uncles, and grandparents, in particular, will be pleased to see the young artist's progress.

Chat Room

Another way to meet on-line is on a family channel. The family creates a "channel" called the King Family, for example. (Relatives must all have the same Internet service provider.) Set a time for those who wish to "talk" and log on no matter where in the world they live. The children can join in, too.

The Greater Family Web Page

Assign an editor-in-chief. Most families have one person who is a good correspondent and is computer literate. Put him or her in charge of designing a greater family web page, collecting news of the entire family, and posting it.

Individuality

Each family within the greater family may wish to create its own home page. The options for web pages that link to the home site are unlimited.

Words alone are becoming obsolete; scan in photographs or videos of the children and vacations, wedding invitations and information, a video of the ceremony for those who missed it, or a child's piano recital. (You always have the option of mailing your videos, too.)

Cribside

You can even, as one family has done, mount a live camera in the baby's crib so visitors to the site will see your new baby in action whenever he's "in residence." There's little reason (other than cost of the equipment) for your extended family not to see your house being built or your children growing up.

More Web Page Options

Build your family web page around your sports or cultural activities, your church, or your genealogy search. Use your web page to sell the family jewels or the sweaters your mother knits. You can add a guestbook sign-in so you know how many people have visited with your family on-line. And you can devise hot links that take the "surfer" directly to the greater family web page.

Privacy Insured

If you wish to keep people other than family off your website, add a secret access password and give it only to family members.

Disintegrating Photo Album

Take your fading or crumbling photo album and old family pictures to cyberspace. Scan the photos onto your website to share with the entire family, wherever they are.

Picture Perfect

Send your 35 mm. roll of film, your 110 roll, or a one-time-use camera to a special lab for processing. The lab will supply you with prints in the size you request as well as make your photos available to you and relatives over the Internet or on a floppy disk.

Computing News

The advent of computers has opened a world of self-publishing that can be manned by the youngest of editors. Software packages set up newsletter pages for you. Fill in the spaces with kernels of personal news and stories and send it off via e-mail. Scanned-in photographs and drawings, even floor plans, will print on paper if you prefer to mail them.

Virtual Congratulations

Log on to the Internet to select greeting cards, postcards, award certificates, virtual junk food, and virtual flowers, which change seasonally, from many different sites as a surprise e-mail for a relative or friend. You can order real flowers on-line, too. Add a personal message and you've acknowledged a special occasion or simply connected in a warm way: "Aunt Bea, you're the greatest." Some sites provide a wide selection of icons to individualize your congratulations, birthday, anniversary, Valentine's, Easter, Halloween, Christmas, or New Year's wishes.

No Excuses

Important occasion reminders are as close as your computer. Register your family's birthdays, anniversaries, and any other dates you want to remember on a special website and you will receive an alert message just before the date. From the reminder message, which is free, you can order greeting cards and an assortment of gifts from flower baskets and chocolates to wines and stuffed animal Easter bunnies (prices vary). These will be delivered anywhere in the United States, and soon worldwide. Some websites offer gift certificates.

ALL TOGETHER NOW—REUNIONS

One of the strongest adhesives in family is being together on a regular basis. Reunions set the stage for seeing family and sharing time under circumstances that are usually relaxed and comfortable.

In some families, reunions began with great-grandparents or grandparents and have been going on for decades. In other families, reunions are novel, begun by siblings or other relatives in recent years.

Family reunions, long in the planning and normally larger in scope than holiday and traditional family celebrations, vary in time of year, place, size, frequency, and flavor. Whatever the mode, whoever the planners, whatever the arrangements, reunions work. Even those who have no apparent attachments, who have never attended their family reunions, or arrive not knowing anyone, leave with good feelings about family.

Parent Pleasing

It may be important to one of your parents that you attend a reunion. "I didn't know anyone, I really didn't want to go, but my father insisted," a reluctant Ross, twenty-nine and single, admits.

"As it turns out, I had the best time. I was so happy I had done it. I have a feeling of being connected to family I didn't have before. And I had a fabulous time."

Same Time Next Year

"Our family reunion is the first weekend in July ever since they started twenty years ago. The fact that it's the same time heightens the anticipation and makes it easier to participate. You know the weekend and can plan to be free," says Andy, who definitely favors the set time.

Mark the Calendar

"My mother calls me every January to be sure I put the August date on my calendar. It's a real expectation. It's okay not to go, but everyone is expected to go," states Ingrid.

Notice in Writing

Keith's family covers the bases further for its July reunion: "We receive a letter in February telling us what hotel has been selected and the dates. In early June a confirming letter arrives with any updated information."

Missing Out

If you miss a reunion, try hard to get to the next one. Reunions keep relationships from lapsing entirely.

Novice Attendee

Anna, in her early fifties, had never been to her family's reunions. After her first one, she remarks: "It was scary, unnerving... somewhat like going back to your twenty-fifth high school reunion. You don't know if they are going to like you, if you are going to fit in. We were the odd family because of my mother's second marriage; we didn't know how the other side of the family would feel about us. After the reunion I knew that my family cared."

One Wonderful Week

A reunion can be one meal on a weekend afternoon or a fully planned event running from Friday through Sunday or longer. "Our reunion, since we are so spread out and have it once every four years, lasts a full week. One wonderful week," is how Madeline describes it.

Sibling-Initiated

"We're five girls and we take turns hosting the reunion. The hostess provides the place," relates Kristen, thirty-one, the youngest sister. "We chip in on the food and invite our children, spouses, our parents, and cousins. The main motive is for the sisters to be together, since we live all over the country.

"We've had our reunion in Maine, on Cape Cod, in Seattle, and in Florida. We're starting over as hostesses because one sister can't afford to lodge us right now."

Business to Pleasure

Turn a business trip into a family reunion by bringing your spouse and children along. Call relatives in the area well in advance and the reunion will take on a life of its own.

Happy Birthday/Happy Anniversary

In some families, significant gatherings such as confirmations, bar and bas mitzvahs, weddings, funerals, and graduations serve as reunions because the number of family in attendance is so large. A relative's commemorative birthday or anniversary is also a fine

"excuse" to bring the family together and substitutes for more formal reunions.

"For my in-laws' fiftieth anniversary, their children had a whole planned weekend," Francine, a sister-in-law, says, and provides the details. "They scheduled square dancing one night, a party another. There were speeches and storytelling at the festivities. No one in the family—with fourteen brothers and sisters, that's about seventy people all tolled—missed it, so it was similar to our summer reunions."

Happy Birthday to All

Celebrate the birthday of relatives who were born in the same month at one time. Celebrate major birthdays—the seventieth birthday of an aunt, the eightieth of an uncle, and the sixty-fifth of a parent in one big party that would include several individual families and all close relations and friends.

A Private Affair

Reunions don't always have to be expansive. Invite your closest family members on a weekend or weeklong trip to celebrate a wedding anniversary or milestone birthday.

Hard Choices

On the one hand, divorce breaks up a family; on the other, it opens possibilities for new family. When a family has many wings, try to attend each branch's reunion or visit one branch for a holiday, another during a vacation.

Circulate

At large family reunions, the tendency is to be with the relatives you know. Make it a point to visit with the relatives you don't see on a regular basis—the ones you only see at the reunion.

Who's Who

Reunions can be very confusing in families with many off-spring, remarriages, and the inclusion of friends. To reduce the confusion, post a huge family tree during the reunion and hand out smaller versions to carry around. Guests can sort out who's who whenever they have time.

Tags

"So you're Jana Jones, daughter of Pamela Jones." Identifying links written on name tags clarify relationships and ease people into conversation. Badges are especially helpful for those who have married into a family.

Use plastic covers with pins or another sturdy form of attachment so reunion guests can wear their identification for the duration of the reunion.

Reunion Rewards

Because of her parents' divorce, Monica was in her early thirties when she attended her first reunion with her father's side of the family. "I didn't know any of my cousins up to that point. What happened is I have about forty 'new' cousins. One set of those cousins flies west to spend weekends and some holidays with us. We didn't even know them five years ago."

Making Reunions Happen

WHEN YOU THINK it's impossible to get your family together, think of Lawrence's scenario and you'll realize that if the desire is there, a get-together can be arranged.

Lawrence recounts: "For our Christmas reunion, the logistics for having the family meet in Florida are:

- My husband, my mother-in-law, and I are flying down from New York.

- My aunt and uncle are flying from Canada.

- Their daughter, son-in-law, and three children are coming from the Midwest via a cruise with…

- My cousin's brother who lives in the south of France.

- Another cousin, his wife, and their children are flying in from Oregon.

- And as the word spreads, whoever wishes is welcome."

Provide a Carrot

"As teenagers, and I remember this from my teens," reminisces Willa, "we were allowed to take a friend. Bringing a friend is the 'carrot' that gets my teenage daughter to join the family."

Planners Needed

A reunion's architects ideally live near each other so they can get together to review and implement plans. Some families elect new coordinators each year at a family meeting held during the reunion.

President-elect

Large families may decide to elect a president and treasurer who are in charge of the reunion and perhaps a secretary to record and send out family news and keep tabs on family members throughout the year. The tenure of office can be determined by how involved the officers are.

"We don't change very often because the president in our family is usually very enthusiastic and the rest of us feel if he or she wants to put the reunion together, he should," notes Barry.

Committee Work

Get-togethers run smoothly if someone or several people have orchestrated activities and prepared or arranged for meals. Committees can be formed at a reunion for the following one or requests for committee members can be mailed or posted on the family web page.

A site committee, for instance, will look for and determine the location of the following reunion. The entertainment committee decides whether or not there will be plays, recitals, or special entertainment. An activities committee can work out the particulars of bike riding, hiking, tennis—perhaps a family tournament—boating, and the like.

Information Sheets

People will be happier and focus on being together if their input is recognized. "As the organizer," delineates Helen, "I send out requests for where people would like to go, what are the best dates for them, what they would most like to do. The sheets include space for food suggestions. If nothing else, what I get back gives me a good place to start."

He Who Lives Farthest

When scheduling a reunion, it's most equitable to work around the schedule of the people who must travel the longest distance. If the Caribbean cousins have the farthest to travel, ask them first to suggest the dates.

Site Selection

Since this happening is designed to be fun for all the generations, be sure the site can accommodate everyone comfortably and that there are things to do that will engage the youngest through the oldest guest, either on the site or close by.

The facility should be equipped to handle a big crowd, if you're having one, with the capability to feed them or a policy that allows you to bring in the food you will need. Many state parks with good campsites, for example, provide the essentials for large groups.

At Home

When the number of people attending is too large for all to stay at one relative's house, use the home for serving meals and activities, but lodge the relatives in local hotels and motels. This way, the family will be together most of the time without feeling cramped.

Host Homes

When a number of families live in the area selected for the reunion, randomly assign quarters for out-of-state family. Part of the fun is staying with and getting to know family members you may not know well.

Finally, Rebellion

"Because of the sheer numbers in our family, our reunion became an enormous chore for those brothers and sisters who live near their parents. Since our reunion begins on Christmas Eve, their holidays were wrecked every year with all the cleaning and cooking and housing of out-of-town siblings and their respective children.

"This year one sister-in-law complained. Most agreed with her that it was too much work. We replaced Christmas Eve and Christmas Day festivities with a huge party in a rented church instead of in one of their homes—on the weekend following Christmas.

Everyone was content. The out-of-town siblings got to spend Christmas at home for the first time in years and the 'locals' didn't have to kill themselves preparing for the onslaught," relates Vivian, one of the formerly descending herds. "We stayed one night instead of the usual two or three."

For Rent

When the reunion gets too big to handle on home ground, rent a private summer camp facility for a day or for the weekend. Some specialty camps have a weekend or two available in the summer between sessions. Stay in the dorms and use their kitchen facilities. Or rent a villa, a couple of log cabins, a public campsite, or motel/hotel rooms.

Moving Around

Those with small families may prefer to move the location each year so that they can experience new parts of the country and try new activities.

No Frills

"We don't plan anything big deal, but my three brothers, their spouses, and children and I usually wind up at my parents' home, which is on the beach," says Holly. "It's just us, no aunts or uncles or second cousins. We love being together. It's fun without the formality and work."

Newsy Alert

Use letters, e-mail, or family web pages to remind everyone. Suggest they bring photos of an interesting trip, a new baby, a wedding, a competition they were in, or pictures of a family event others may have missed.

Teasers

As a reunion draws near, send out a bulletin with "teaser" information about expected guests: Will Jennifer Hall have her baby at the reunion? Is Cousin Dilys going to have her next book ready for us to read? Will Uncle Jim be engaged? Will Aunt Janet be fully trained for the marathon?

You can build a frenzy of excitement about a reunion with tantalizing tidbits and engaging questions.

We Like This Place

It may be that someone in your family lives in an area conducive to large gatherings, one that also provides the opportunity for different activities. This "great place" can be someone's home, a hotel, a resort area with pony rides for the children, a lake, a beach, mountains to climb, or rivers to fish in. If it works and the family is in agreement, your reunion can be held there year after year.

"For as long as I can remember," comments Willa, the mother of a teenage son, "every August we packed the car and drove up the mountain to the picnic. Eating goes on all day—chicken and hamburgers continually coming off the grill.

"People sit around and eat and talk and walk in the woods. There's a large lake for boating and looking for beaver; some people swim, some fish. I've been going there since I was a very young child. It's like a sacred place."

Ideal Surroundings

Have you located an idyllic reunion, camping, or vacation spot? Tell family and friends about it, even if you can't be there to enjoy it with them.

Money Matters

PAYING REUNION EXPENSES poses a problem in many families. Here are ways to handle money matters, from charging a nominal fee to one large enough to pay airfare and reunion expenses for family members who would otherwise be unable to attend.

Support

In most nuclear families, relatives know who has money and who doesn't at any given point. Volunteer to pay for a sibling, parent, or cousin who can't.

The Fund

In order to have everyone who wants to be there present, start a travel fund supported by those who can afford to contribute. Choose a family treasurer to decide who will receive airline tickets and have their accommodations paid for by the fund. At the reunion remind everyone that the fund accepts or needs donations for next year.

Fund-raisers

To raise money for the kitty, families sell T-shirts or hats printed to represent a family get-together.

"One year we printed the family line on T-shirts so people could see from whom they had descended. The design was like a tree, with a leaf here and there," says Amanda, the shirt's designer and a graphic artist.

Selling family cookbooks, family histories in book form, or family videotapes is another good way to raise money to partially fund a reunion.

No Options

The reunion is one of the few times immediate family can be together and your children can see their cousins. If you send your children—and grandchildren—airline tickets, make sure these tickets are not exchangeable for a trip elsewhere.

Reserved

Have the family treasurer or someone assigned to the job of collecting a small fee—a few dollars or more, depending on the size of your family or the cost of the place—from each person to reserve special or preferred facilities for the next year's reunion.

Reunion Club

Like a Christmas Club at the bank, put what you can afford away each week or month so that you and your family can afford the expense of traveling to your family reunion. Open a separate savings account to hold the money.

Our Representative

One way to beat the money hurdle is to send one person from your immediate family as your representative. Nina sends one of her teenage children: "I arm him or her with photos and remind her of everything that's happened in our family since the last reunion. Our representative is expected to take lots of pictures and to give a detailed report on her return."

Building Tradition and Memories

Memory makers are places and events as well as people woven into your reunion experiences. Some become annual traditions, others warm memories of good times with family.

A memory can be of kayaking on a small wooded lake or a hole-in-one at the miniature golf course at age ten. It can be the four-leaf clovers you found in a field with your brother-in-law or a cousin you met for the first time the same day. It can be playing dolls when you were seven years old or sinking ball after ball in a basketball game when you were fifty-five. It can be tasting your grandmother's bread pudding for the first time or turning apples you picked into pies.

You may look back decades later with laughter at the fight you had with a sibling or cousin over what now is frightfully insignificant. In short, with family, there's no way to tell what will be remembered. With very little effort you and your relatives will have lots to select from in the reunion recollection department. Getting together in and of itself is a wonderful family tradition.

More than Memories

You can build a whole tradition around what you take from the reunion spot. Pick huckleberries, apples, raspberries, or strawberries. Take them back to bake pies or make jam. As children grow up, they will recall their grandmother or mother, along with cousins and aunts, picking fruit and creating wonderful things to eat.

Family Meeting

At some point during the reunion the family meets as an entire group—for breakfast one morning, after dinner one evening, or during the meal if the reunion is a few hours' event. The family meeting is an ideal time to put on a skit or play. If your family has no president, randomly select someone to lead this gathering.

Genealogy for Breakfast

The tendency is to think that young people are not interested in genealogy, but young and old alike will attend an after-breakfast genealogical session, if you make it amusing and short. Or, use the time to exchange genealogical information, especially if one or two relatives are searching the Internet for family connections.

Telling Tales

Ask each guest to tell a story he or she remembers about any member of the family or an adventure with a parent or grandparent, a cousin or sibling. Life's tales reveal interesting and humorous things about family.

Special Privileges

Set aside an area—a tent, a room, a table—for the seniors in your group to congregate. They may want a separate lunch or dinner or to spend time together in the late afternoon talking about their travels, children, volunteer work, and social activities.

Historic Moments

"My mother shows videos of my brothers and me when we were kids. My children and my nieces and nephews love to see their parents as youngsters," laughs Ralph.

Videos of early reunions will also entertain and bring back old memories for the adults in attendance.

Show and Tell

"People tote mementos every year, and after the meal whoever brought something gets up and tells a story about the item,

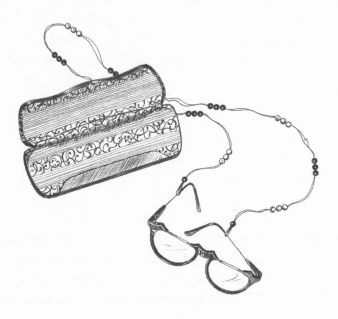

emphasizing its specific connection to the family." Max describes items that have been presented at his reunions:

"Great-grandmother's eyeglasses in a delicate case with a water-silk lining that had been specially purchased in New Orleans and had come up the Mississippi River by steamboat and overland to northeastern Missouri. My cousin offered a very romantic tale about an exquisite pair of eyeglasses.

"One relative brought an odd section of harness for draft horses and asked if anyone knew what it was. We also had decorative clothing and lots of pictures.

"Readings from my Great-aunt Stella's diary were the most amusing. Her love life wasn't all that dissimilar from what goes on in relationships today."

Women's Night Out

"During our week's reunion," reports Roberta, "the men baby-sit, or 'kid-sit,' while the adult women go out to dinner or for an evening's entertainment, like a local play or concert."

Men's Night Out

Reverse the procedure.

Costume Party

Select a theme, such as countries of the world; the Wild West; the sixties; patriotism (everyone dresses in red, white, and blue); or going to the ball. Ask guests to dress for one meal in costume or schedule a costume party as the main reunion event.

Going Formal and Fancy

If you've taken the trouble to dress up, have a photographer record the elegance.

Clambake

Bring everyone to the beach for a shore dinner, but be sure to include foods children will eat. Add a band in the early evening or entertainment by family members. You can hire the local high school group or a fresh, aspiring rock group to keep teens interested.

Family Olympics

Whether a reunion-goer is four years old or seventy-four, organize "Olympic Games" in which they can participate: a walk for the older folks; a mountain climb for the young; two-legged races for the children. You've got the picture.

Treasure Hunt

A willing relative can plan a treasure hunt that lasts an entire afternoon. Or if time is limited, a half-hour treasure hunt can be just as absorbing. Mix families and age groups and send them on their way.

Because photos are effortlessly and inexpensively reproduced on copy machines, a fitting prize is a duplicate of an old family photo album. Candy prizes will satisfy children. Wrap the candy in fun bags or fill inexpensive piggy banks or baskets.

Bike Ride En Masse

Plan a long, leisurely bike ride for everyone in attendance. Have relatives bring their bicycles or rent them. Tricycles, too.

Grab a Partner

Plan an evening of square dancing. All ages can join in. Remind reunion-goers to pack their jeans and bandannas.

For Children Only

Some families have one or more adults who will enjoy taking the children on adventures or involving them in projects. Some suggestions:

- Dig for clams on the beach or build sand castles.

- Collect seashells or heart-shaped rocks.

- Go fishing in a stream.

- Finger paint on a picnic table.

Sports for Everyone

Reserve an indoor sports park with sufficient facilities for the whole family—miniature golf, basketball, tennis, racquetball, perhaps a pool. Then reconnoiter for a potluck or planned lunch.

Family Crest

Have the children design a family crest for themselves or for each adult who is at the reunion. The "winning" crest can later be made into a T-shirt design or pin to hand out at the next reunion.

Family Song

Write it together or have the more talented or inclined relatives try their hand at writing a song. Include humorous happenings and happy events that have taken place in your family.

Reunion Ritual

Have each reunion guest—or one person from each individual family—share something that happened since the last reunion.

Logging Reunion Memories

Remember This One?

Repeat ghost stories that have been passed down from generation to generation. Record them.

History Being Made

Take a picture of the entire clan in attendance each year. Then break the group into individual family units. You'll be able to see the children grow up as you look back on your pictorial history.

No One Missed

Find a charming location—a front door, a wide tree trunk, a beautiful stone wall, an old gate. Line up those present and have them enter or appear, one by one, in front of the video camera. Ask them to say a few words as they pass by.

Send a copy of the videotape to everyone who was there or to each individual family.

Hamming It Up

Take action photos of the children engaged in activities throughout the reunion. Capture them at their silliest and most serious. You also may want to pose the children together—in costume or around a completed sand castle or just eating at a picnic table.

An Album, Just as Good

Assemble a photo album and have it photocopied so each person has his own reunion memory book.

Pass the Album

Put family photos in albums for sharing. Bring along your grandparents' or great-grandparents' photo albums.

At Your Age

"We've had reunions at our home for the past thirty years," reminisces Mae. "Each year I take lots of informal pictures and put together an album to represent what we did and who was there. Now I say to the children, 'Look, here is your mother when she was your age.'"

Better than a Rental

Take snippets of old home movies, including those of people who are no longer alive, and string them together by transferring them to videotape. Rent a television and show home movies of past generations. Make copies of the tape for anyone in the family who would like one.

Remembrance of Reunions Past

Send guests, especially the children, home with a small remembrance that they are likely to keep. In addition to photo albums and videos, consider a picture frame to hold that year's reunion photo, a clay dish or vase made during an activity, a box with the reunion date on its lid, or a mouse pad with the family tree, an old family picture, or one of the children involved in a reunion game or activity.

CHILD CONNECTIONS

We build family on memories. For children, you never know: The most unusual *or* the most commonplace incident can be the one cherished forever. The most unlikely events have a way of becoming part of family lore. But certain approaches and attitudes will surely result in children feeling attached and sustain their desire to be with family as adults. If what you and your children do with family is upbeat and positive, it's safe to assume that family and its favored traditions will prevail and remain a priority.

Anticipation

Let children know how much you look forward to seeing relatives. Get ready happily and with enthusiasm for visits and other planned times together. Your children will pick up on your excitement.

Welcome Mat

Hang signs over the doorway and in the house to welcome out-of-town relatives. It's a great way to say "we're so glad you're here" whatever the relatives' ages. And to children a welcoming gesture underscores just how you feel.

Put Feelings into Words

Point out how much fun an uncle is, the interesting or risky work a cousin performs, the twists and turns an aunt's life has taken. Encourage your children to ask a relative about an unusual experience or trip that person has taken.

Role Model

Go out of your way to be with relatives. Begin taking the children along when they are babies so they grow up knowing their grandparents, aunts, uncles, and cousins.

Perfect Turns

"When my niece was sixteen and learning to drive, her parents were reluctant to put her behind the wheel," recalls Mia. "What's more important to a teen than her driver's license? I steeled myself and took her to a quiet neighborhood to practice her skills. That's what aunts are for, I told myself.

"Her roadblock to driving success was right turns. She simply couldn't make them. But no matter how wide or how close to the curb or a parked car she turned, I smiled and said, 'Perfect.' Confidence building, I believe, is an aunt's mission.

"Later that evening I insisted that my niece could drive the entire family home from dinner. I continued saying 'Perfect,' at each right turn. We were hysterical at her near misses, and to this day we say 'Perfect,' whenever my niece, who is thirty, turns the wheel into one of her now infamous—at least in our family—right turns."

Caring Conveyed

At exam time send college or high school students a small memento—a box of cookies or an assortment of food you know they enjoy, a bunch of soaps, a new CD—with a note that says, "I know this is a hard time for you."

Instant Recognition

Acknowledge childhood milestones with a card, an inexpensive toy, trinket, or a stuffed animal.

I Thought of You

Subscribe to a magazine you know a child in your family would like. Send an article or book about something that interests her. Write a note to tell her about someone in your town who is doing the same thing she is.

Postcard Collection

Postcards are ideal for keeping children informed of your travels—be they business trips, pleasure trips, or both. Make a point to send one from every place you visit as well as some from your hometown. Let the receivers know that you are starting a postcard collection for them. They'll be looking for your mail even if they are too young to read it.

Direct Questions

Today it's unrealistic for most children to walk to their relatives' homes and stop in to visit with them. As an adult, asking questions involves you in the child's life, no matter how far away you live.

Find out directly how a youngster in the family did on a recent test, her college entrance exams, in a Little League game, a tennis tournament, an art or poetry contest.

A Sense of Family

You can create a lasting sense of family through repetition—the same house for Thanksgiving, the same relatives invited to a child's family birthday party, vacations with the same relatives. Henry, who is ten years old, says his family reunion "is the highlight of my year."

Children are not as aware of the long-range impact of being with their relatives. For most children, family experiences have more to do with the fun of the moment, but each family happening is another link in the chain that is the bridge to family.

Keeping Heritage Intact

The often divisive element of divorce separates family members from access to relatives they have known for years or just a few years. For children who are too young to make their own arrangements, it's wise to retain those ties and be sure they see relatives they could so easily lose touch with. When a parent denies such access, they are in fact denying their children's heritage.

Something New...

...Or something a parent can't or doesn't want to do will turn you into a hero or heroine. Go sledding, fix a broken window or toy, build a tree house, or equip a tank to house the lizards and frogs you find together. Teach your niece or nephew how to bait a hook or cast a fishing line.

Extend Yourself

When time together with young relatives is limited, plan to make what you do child-centered and enjoyable. Visit museums with volcanoes or insects, a water park, or the zoo. Create train-set cities or design a phenomenal building with blocks. Making children the focus makes them feel special and especially attached to you.

Uncle Dan—Gourmet Chef

Whatever your specialty—be it cooking or knitting, glass-blowing, guitar playing, or gardening—introduce young relatives by allowing them to assist or participate in the activity.

Instant Camaraderie

If you've always adored your sister or brother, an aunt or uncle, he or she will usually be genuinely flattered if you choose to name a child after him. Ask first. Some, although they're the exception, are very protective of their names.

About You

Most children love to hear stories about a parent's childhood. Tell yours weaving in humorous incidents that happened with *your* cousins—your children's aunts and uncles—or *your* parents and grandparents. They will ask to have the funniest and most adventuresome tales repeated frequently.

The Homestead

Children's curiosity extends to physical places, too. They will want you to take them to the city or town you grew up in and to see your home. Ideally, it still exists, perhaps in an unrecognizable state. Point out which bedroom was yours and, if you can obtain access, describe the wallpaper and furnishings as you remember them. Talk about how the neighborhood used to be.

For Him or Her

"We made a video for our children that began before they were born," explain Linda and Denton. "The video was not about them, but *for them*. We included our house and interesting things about it; we taped all the relatives and close friends and points of interest in the town. I'm sure for others it's a bit like seeing someone else's travel video, but for the children it will be their tie to their early life and family."

Fringe Benefits

Visit siblings who live in different parts of the country. Visiting different places is an opportunity to introduce children to other ways of life if you reside in a big city and a sibling lives on a farm or in a small town—and vice versa.

Sum, Sum, Summertime

An option for children is to spend the summer or part of it with relatives. You can send your child for a week or weekend visit with an older step-sibling, aunts, uncles, cousins, or grandparents. Children can attend the same camp or take the same trip. Or visit an aging relative as a family.

Being Thankful

Go around the dinner table and ask everyone to say what they are thankful for. Many comments will include "being together" and subtly reinforce family connections for children.

Framed

Frame family holiday or trip photos and hang them in your home. Put photos of children with their cousins and other relatives in their rooms.

Pass It On

Your old hockey stick, tennis racquet, fishing pole, your first set of tools or cookbook, whatever...pass it on to the next generation for his or her use, or to have the honor of keeping it for you.

Share Your Energy

Be a bit outrageous, full of childlike enthusiasm. Let children feel your energy whether you're their parent, grandparent, aunt, uncle, older cousin, or family friend. Outgoing children are likely to attach to fun-loving adults and older children.

Be Yourself

On the other hand, shy, quiet children may relate best to the relative who is calm and comforting. So, be yourself, but whatever your approach, engage the young set in conversation, an excellent foundation for blossoming bonds.

Shirt Off His Back

As a reminder of the fun you had, lend your niece, nephew, or a younger cousin a cap or sweatshirt of yours that he or she fancies. Perhaps it's your baseball bat or raft. It might be a purse, a sweater, or a rabbit's foot.

We'll Have Two

Buying a souvenir or ordering food, ask for two—one for yourself and one for that young relative who looks up to you.

You may have to point out to teenagers that a younger cousin is admiring them.

Team Play

Grace makes suggestions for cousin bonding: "My sister and I have many routines that make sharing a vacation house with eleven people pleasant. We set up teams for all the chores—cooking, cleaning, shopping. Age is insignificant and don't put siblings on the same team. We put the oldest boy cousin with the youngest girl cousin.

"The adults have their own teams, but fill in for a child that the other children don't want to be with because that unwanted child refuses to do the work or can't. Teams are usually two people, sometimes three. Early on, team spirit takes over," continues Grace, "and each team wants to serve a great meal. The cooks tend to cook together; the noncooks keep it simple."

Less than Subtle

Boastful toasts and speeches of praise at family parties and dinners are good ways for children to learn of their relatives' strong points, accomplishments, and feats.

Roses Are Red…

…Violets are blue.
This poem was written
especially for you.

The customary holiday ritual in many large families is to pick a name out of a hat and that's the person for whom you buy a Christmas or Hanukkah gift. Instead of purchasing a gift, write a poem. When presents would normally be opened, the recipient or the giver reads the poem aloud to the assembled group.

The youngest of children can participate with a little help from older siblings or a parent. If you pull the name of a child or in-law you don't know enough about, call his or her parent, spouse, or child to fill you in. This is a humorous, memorable way to learn about family members and have a potentially hilarious holiday celebration year after year.

Month by Month

To underscore caring, fill in wall calendars each month with relatives' and friends' birthdays and anniversaries. Have the children call with warm wishes and be sure you ask them to make or sign celebratory cards.

The Green Bay Packers

You must be under twenty-one to be eligible for the prize. Draw up a football pool letting children know what quarter and team they have; create a "kitty" of age-appropriate prizes—stuffed animals, miniature footballs, team hats or mugs, candy.

Show Your Emotions

Express your feelings about family. Tell a cousin or niece you enjoy spending time with her. Expound with positive comments to your own children after being with relatives.

Caring Is Contagious

Be kind, caring, and concerned about family. Take turns helping a sibling or relative who is needy. Children will see you shopping, taking the relative to the doctor, keeping him or her company. When it isn't your turn, call to make sure everything is okay.

Calling All Cousins

Put the children on the telephone with each other at early ages. They find things to talk about—the latest computer game, the newest television series.

"My brother-in-law put the cousins on the phone when they were still too young to dial," acknowledges Elana. "That well may have been the beginning of the cousin's good feelings about each other. All four are college students and check in with each other on a regular basis. And I support the telephone company—big time."

E-mail, however, is a relatively inexpensive way for cousins to pass information back and forth.

Prepared

Send school-age children their own copies of your family tree. It may not be important to them when they are children or adolescents, but as they get older, they will become more curious about where they came from. And they'll be prepared: Many teachers request family heritage information and you will be giving the children in your family a major head start on whatever family history project is assigned.

Recording Connections

Give children spiral notebooks or pads of paper and ask them to write down or draw pictures of their thoughts about a family get-together, an outing, an adventure. They can share them or not. The very organized will keep comments in the same place from event to event, from year to year.

STERLING OPPORTUNITIES

Traditionally, in most families, holidays such as Thanksgiving, Christmas, and Passover are convenient times for congregating. But there are many, many other chances to be together. When an opportunity presents itself or a situation exists to relate to family or friends, seize it. Some occasions present themselves only once. What you may believe to be a chore or "command performance" sometimes delivers unexpected surprises.

Kid-sitting

Invited to care for her two young nephews for a week while her brother and sister-in-law were on vacation, Carrie was concerned: "A whole week without my gym, without my computer. My diet will go down the drain and I'll have to drive them to the mall," she moaned. A serious dieter and an infrequent driver, Carrie was nervous but agreed.

The aftermath: "I had the best time. I got to know those boys and love them even more. I didn't even short them—or myself—on junk food. I dieted when I returned home," she says, pleased with her decision.

Reenlisting

Jack suggested maybe he had missed out. "As a child I was very involved with family. But, as an adult, I lived away from my family and lost contact with most of them. It wasn't until I retired and moved back to their part of the country that I reentered the family. At this late date, they still made me feel included and welcome."

Homeward Bound

Once you've located your ancestral home, plan a trip. It's more than an adventure to go back in time to a city—most likely in another country—in which your relatives once lived. No doubt it's changed, but as Terrence feels, "It's reinforcing to be able to plant your feet on the same soil as your ancestors."

To the Archives

Combine a family reunion with an ancestral search one year. The whole family can be involved in looking up names, birth certificates, marriage licenses, and property titles in local records. You will probably discover relatives you never knew about.

Observing Holidays Is a Draw

Use a holiday, be it Purim or Easter, Christmas or Hanukkah to pull family together. Kathryn has been doing so for decades: "When I was pregnant with my first child and in a mixed marriage, I decided that we needed one religion. I chose to convert and spent a great deal of time learning the holidays and rituals of my husband's religion," explains Kathryn. "We have become a central force in our family as a result. Holidays, because they have become a happening, bring sixty or more family members to our home for dinner."

Going Abroad

Travel to meet family that you don't know or look them up if you are there on business or vacation. Language won't be as great a barrier as you might expect. You'll make yourselves understood through gestures, pictures, and their broken English.

Make the Most

Make the most of every visit from relatives. Pack it full of events and invite other family members to dinner or on excursions you plan for your out-of-town or out-of-the-country visitor.

Relationship Renewed

Anytime is a good time to mend or improve a strained relationship. Even a family death can be the trigger you need to heal old wounds. Ask personal questions to show your interest.

"When our father died," points out Krista, "something clicked in my sister, and our relationship became closer than it ever was. Where once she had no idea what colleges my sons attend, she became curious about their well-being, my business, my husband—everything important to me."

One Thing Leads to Another

"What amazed me at my father's funeral was the huge number of family members who came great distances to be there, and the outpouring of love that I don't think you can get on the outside. It made me appreciate my family in a different way, and it also made me realize I had neglected them for many years," laments Sterling.

"We are in more contact since Dad's death than we were before. The funeral made me see that I had to do something to keep the family together. We began that very summer to have an annual family reunion."

SPECIAL LINKS

YOU CAN'T FORCE a relationship, but one may develop if you extend yourself just a bit. Be it a birth or adoption, an elementary or high school graduation, or college acceptance, there are endless occasions—some of which you may want to invent—to link up with relatives and friends and remind them of your bond.

I Do

Weddings are as important as funerals. Holding weddings in unusual places may tempt more family members to attend. Similarly, unusual wedding themes will attract family members as do less formal weddings. Or plan to have the wedding at the same or a nearby location and on the same weekend as the family reunion.

On the Grill

Use summer as an excuse to bring everyone—or a few—together for a barbecue. No major celebration needed.

Scrapbook Collage

Send a blank scrapbook page to each guest invited to an important celebration—a wedding, an anniversary, or a "big" birthday. Instructions accompanying the page: Fill the page in any way you wish: Celebrate the recipient with a poem, a drawing, a cartoon, photographs, a letter extolling his or her personality, or anything that relates to the life of the person or couple who will "own" the completed scrapbook. Have pages returned to you for assembling.

Facials, Back Rubs, Manicures

Patti takes pleasure in her sisters' annual slumber party. "There are five sisters and seven nieces who come along with their mothers. We talk and eat, tell jokes, do each other's hair and makeup, and have a great time acting like we did when we were teenagers.

Good Old Days

Find an old photo of you and the special person you want to reminisce with, celebrate with, or honor. Choose a picture that represents a good time you had together. The framed original or a copy will be a reminder of the good old days and is a thoughtful and unique gift.

A Style of Their Own

Greg's family and his wife's family maximize being together. However, Greg differentiates: "When Kay's family meets, they spend their time talking and catching up. In my family, it's activities. At nine o'clock we set out to do this; at eleven, we're doing that. It's nonstop motion rather than just eating and hanging out."

Indigenous

"When our relatives visit we try to find something that is native to our area or can only be seen here. The Kennedy Museum is a must stop in Dallas. We took some of them horseback riding. That's very Texas," remarks Dallas-born-and-bred Harris.

The Usefulness of Aunts

Loving includes letting go and saying, "You do your own thing now."

"That's one of the reasons I stay in close touch with my nieces," says Georgia. "I can see when they're trying to break loose from their mothers. There are struggles, yet the girls still need to be in touch with some female in the family who can appreciate them the way they are and let them make their own stupid mistakes.

"Mothers can't help identifying with children's blunders and trying to stop them. As an aunt I can just be understanding; I'm not responsible for them. When they're on the outs with their mothers, I'm that crucial somebody to talk to."

Progress Report

A pending birth or adoption of a baby is a good reason to contact the family member you may not see or speak with on a regular basis. Call to find out how the adoption process is moving along or to hear the latest pregnancy report.

Spreading the News

When something wonderful happens to you, a relative, or a friend, announce it. Make a call, write a note, or send an e-mail to let everyone know about that job promotion, new addition to the family, award or honor, child's milestone met, or relocation.

Surprise Package

Cleaning up or moving? Pack up old toys and memorabilia and ship them off to their "rightful" owner or a family member who you think will appreciate them. Include a grandparent's or great-grandparent's photo, cane, or hat, along with your child's or sister's favored children's book or baby cup.

Many Talents

Be an instructive or helping hand for members of your family, young and old. Choose entertainments and projects that are your strong suit and invite family members to join you. It could be sailing, mountain climbing, or building a birdhouse. You may be a great baseball player or pianist. Perhaps you can help a relative train the dog, find his or her way around the Internet, or fix a leaky faucet. Whatever your forte, share it.

"I have relatives who do just about anything I might need," says Jenna. "In my family there's a dentist, a writer, a vet, a carpenter, a painter, a plumber, and a doctor. I take advantage," she adds, with a smile.

Just Moved

Don't wait for the house to be in perfect order. Invite family and friends to help you unpack. An unpacking party speeds up getting settled, reduces your workload, and turns what can be an overwhelming chore into one that is manageable, memorable, and fun.

Conversation Piece

The bookends your brother carved, the ceramic bowl you "turned" for your father's desk decades ago, or your mother's perfume bottles are daily reminders of family ties when displayed on a shelf in your home. They are also wonderful conversation starters for telling children and visitors about family.

Gone Fishing

Plan an annual boating or ski trip with a sister, brother, or friend. Arrange to visit a new city each year or attend an out-of-town business meeting, county fair, or event that is of interest to both of you.

Climbers Connect

Tackle the local mountain or go for a big one with the experienced climbers in the family or among your friends. Ask, and you may be surprised to discover that you have relatives with the same leanings.

Hats Off to Us

Hand out printed hats with the date of a family event or T-shirt with a picture of a place you vacationed. Either is a useful reminder of your bond when you are not together.

The Singing Sensations

Sing around the table at Thanksgiving, at parties, outside in the summer. Personalize songs for birthdays, weddings, and anniversaries. Make up congratulation songs for special achievements.

Prepare a song for anyone new who comes to visit. It doesn't always have to be original—a city or state song, a college song or show tune that somehow relates will do. The song is meant as a welcoming, to bring newcomers in to the family—new spouses, new in-laws, new friends.

The Gift of Family

When you need a gift for a relative, think family. A video of your children for aunts and uncles or an ancestor's curio or gadget will always be well received and treasured. Gifts of family are sterling ways to underscore connections.

Happy Mother's Day

For Mother's or Father's Day have an old snapshot of you as a child with your parent reprinted and put it in a frame. You can scan it into your computer or at a copy center and move the image and the background.

Twelve Months of Family

As a Christmas or New Year's gift for family members, collect twelve family photos—some old, some recent. A copy center can put them together into bound calendars, as many as you need. If you know family members' birthdays, planned holiday and reunion gatherings, add them before the calendars are printed.

Just Deal 'Em

Have a cherished family photograph, your child's school picture, or images of your pet put onto a deck of cards to give to card-playing relatives.

This Is Your Life

For the person—relative or friend—most dear to you, gather photographs of his or her life and arrange them in chronological order for a very special occasion. If time permits, add captions.

Lasting Connections

Family is a lifetime connection. It gives you a sense of not being alone, of belonging. Similarities in beliefs, in taste, or in appearance not only secure the attachment but also tell you who you are. Beyond that, family—be it immediate or extended, and whatever its makeup or size—can be the most supportive and loving element in your life.

Friends as Family

Extending extended family to encompass those out of the bloodline provides another opportunity for children and adults to feel part of a larger whole.

In today's world the concept of family often includes friends who live nearby. Godparents, frequently not relatives, are chosen because they will play an active role in a child's life.

Stand-Ins

Children become devoted to those they see most often. They may begin to call your close friends "Aunt" and "Uncle." These friends watch your child grow; they are aware of the many wonderful, sometimes small, achievements that are so important to a child and his parents—academic recognition, sports accolades, parties, proms.

"I grew up calling our neighbors Aunt and Uncle. They knew more about what we did than my real aunts and uncles, who are spotted about the country," points out Phillip. "At my sister's wedding, an usher asked our neighbors, 'Which side of the family?' in order to seat them on the proper side. They looked at each other and said, 'The bride's, of course. We're her aunt and uncle.'"

Filling the Voids

Beyond liking them, you choose close friends because they serve you in a variety of ways. Extended family members are comforting when your family is too far away to see regularly, makes you unhappy, or is no longer alive. These friends are supportive in ways parents and siblings are.

Substitute Support

Support your extended family and/or "friend family" by filling in as a substitute mom, dad, or absent grandparent at sporting events, the school play, or spring concert—even on visiting day at camp.

Best Friend

"She's the closest person in the world to me," notes Donna. "I imagine it's the relationship some people have with a sister, but I only have a brother."

"Family" Vacations

Take an annual vacation with a friend, her children, and your children. It can be an extended camping trip each year or a day trip to see the sights in a nearby city. As children get older, they will have stronger opinions on where they want to go and what they want to do, and will want more of a say in deciding the destination.

On Display

As with family photographs, give and display pictures with close friends that reflect your history together.

Thanks for Stopping By

Visit a friend's parents when you have time. If you've been friends for decades, you're "family" enough to drop in occasionally to bolster the spirits of a friend's aging or infirm parent.

The More the Merrier

For reasons of size and geographical distance, many families have the desire to enlarge the group, especially for the children and especially around holidays. Include extended family and close friends for these celebrations.

Dividing Time

"My stepmother and father invite three sets of friends and the friends' children for Christmas Eve," explains Seth. "It has been this way all our lives; it's an event none of us misses, even now as young adults. Other than parents and siblings, there are no relatives. We celebrate Christmas Day with family."

Reinforcing Friendship

To lengthen the holidays, attend services with a friend and her family of another faith. Experiencing a friend's religion strengthens bonds and "makes us more tolerant of each other," expresses Yolanda.

The Keys to Lasting Connections

FAMILY IS A CONTINUUM made up of the generations before and the generations that will come after. You have a place on the continuum and a responsibility. Being enthusiastic about your family is perhaps the best way to keep family alive.

As one woman noted, "The people I like the best, that I enjoy being with happen to be my relatives." If you have a wonderful relationship with one or several of your relatives, you'll find ways to nurture it.

Not allowing important relationships to wane and carrying on family tradition once the older generation is gone certainly play a part, but enthusiasm makes the rest happen.

Division of Labor

When it doesn't all fall to one person, more happens to keep us close. Spread the responsibility by asking others to make the phone calls, check on a relative's health, or spread the "good news."

Acceptance

People are naturally different. Once you decide you can't change people in your family, you'll be able to enjoy or at the least accept them as they are.

Looking the Other Way

There are times it's just best to ignore what annoys you in a relative. "I don't like my sister-in-law," says Bob. "But if I start picking out all her flaws to my brother, it will ruin my relationship with him, both their relationships with my children, and all the children's relationships with each other. I'm cordial and I keep my mouth shut to keep relations amiable."

Remembering

Remember birthdays with a card or note. Cards make young children feel like kings for the day and older people feel loved and important.

Beyond the Gift

Connections are so much more rewarding when they go beyond a present in the mail at Christmas followed by a thank-you note. Make a point to be in touch at other times during the year. Jot a note to yourself in your calendar as a reminder.

Your Choice

If you have no strong feelings about a name, allow a grandparent or other relative to name your child. You may want to put some parameters on the naming, or better yet, give the selector a limited number of choices.

Rough Times

Offer a service or your time to a relative in need.

Thoughtfulness

Consider what would please a person most, then do it. It can be supplying a simple exercise or cleaning tip or more involved, like this one: "The way to my brother's heart is through his stomach," Gloria told her new sister-in-law. Gloria wrote out, boxed, and gift-wrapped her brother's favorite recipes that their mother used to make and handed them to her sister-in-law on her wedding day.

Building Trust

You build a sense of trust when you are open about problems with those closest to you. They are the ones who will be most supportive if they know you are having difficulties. They, in turn, will feel comfortable coming to you when they need support.

Personal Enjoyment

Your attachment to one or several family members can be as simple as having fun together. "One of my cousins and I run together. We alternate being the leader and do not tell the other person the planned route. It's exciting to follow and not know exactly where you'll end up." Bruce contends that this "follow-the-leader" routine is one of the reasons he and his cousin are so close. "A male-bonding ritual, of sorts," he adds.

Insights

Make an effort to visit relatives in their own surroundings. Seeing people on their home turf often explains a lot and will help you understand them.

Welcoming

Being friendly and open is a major plus when greeting and meeting relatives. The relatives with the most appeal to other family members seem to be the ones who are welcoming and inclusive. Whenever you are together, ask a relative to join you on a walk so you can talk and get to know each other better.

Continued Interest

Carry your interest in someone between visits by remembering what she said last time you were together. If appropriate, ask questions about a plan, goal, or project she said she was involved in or going to do.

Caring

Caring is the essential ingredient. With caring comes the desire to be more than relatives—to be friends as well. You can't force friendship, but you can provide a fertile ground in which it flourishes. You now have the tools with which to accomplish that goal.

Today's the Day

Next time you think or say "One of these days I'm going to get in touch with or get together with...," make that day today. After all, family and good friends are forever.